I0483741

Indoor Air Quality in Commercial and Institutional Buildings

Occupational Safety and Health Administration
U.S. Department of Labor

OSHA 3430-04
2011

U.S. Department of Labor
Hilda L. Solis, Secretary of Labor

Contents

Introduction

Indoor air quality (IAQ) is a major concern to businesses, schools, building managers, tenants, and workers because it can impact the health, comfort, well-being, and productivity of the building occupants. OSHA recognizes that poor IAQ can be hazardous to workers' health and that it is in the best interest of everyone that building owners, managers, and employers take a proactive approach to address IAQ concerns.

This OSHA guidance document on IAQ provides practical recommendations that will help prevent or minimize IAQ problems in commercial and institutional buildings, and help resolve such problems quickly if they do arise. It provides flexible guidance to employers to help them keep their buildings free of pollutants or conditions that lead to poor IAQ. It also provides information on good IAQ management, including control of airborne pollutants, introduction and distribution of adequate make-up air, and maintenance of an acceptable temperature and relative humidity. Temperature and humidity are important because thermal comfort underlies many complaints about "poor air quality." Some of the information presented here has been derived from the Environmental Protection Agency's (EPA) report, "*An Office Building Occupant's Guide to IAQ*" (1)[1] and other documents listed in Appendix E, Selected Resources. The issue of environmental tobacco smoke will only be addressed in Appendix F, or indirectly in discussions of air quality relative to some possible components of tobacco smoke, e.g., carbon monoxide, carbon dioxide, particulates, etc. In 1998, OSHA conducted a series of three workshops on this issue and the proceedings of these workshops were published in 1999. See Appendix F for more information.

This document is directed primarily at employers, building owners and managers, and others responsible for building maintenance, but may also be used as a basic reference for all those involved in IAQ issues. Furthermore, information presented here can help with the decision of whether or not the services of an outside professional may be needed. The advice of a medical professional should always be sought if there are any immediate health issues. Contractors and other professionals (e.g., industrial hygienists or other environmental health and safety professionals) who respond to IAQ concerns, as well as members of the general public, may also find this information helpful.

[1]The numbers in parentheses refer to specific entries in the last section of this document titled "References."

Background

IAQ has been identified by the EPA as one of the top five most urgent environmental risks to public health (2). The Centers for Disease Control and Prevention (CDC) estimates that the majority of Americans spend approximately 90 percent of their time indoors (3). On average, office workers spend approximately 40 hours a week in office buildings. These workers also study, eat, drink, and, in certain work settings, sleep in enclosed environments where make-up air (i.e., fresh air added to re-circulated air) may be compromised. For this reason, some experts believe that more people may suffer from the effects of indoor air pollution than from outdoor air pollution.

Each building has its own set of circumstances. Air quality may be determined by the site of the building, its original design, renovations, whether air handling systems have been maintained, occupant densities, activities conducted within the building, and the occupants' satisfaction with their environment. IAQ problems can arise from a single source or any combination of factors. Inadequate IAQ may begin with poor building design or failure of the building enclosure or envelope (roof, facade, foundation, etc.). Other issues may be associated with the location of the building and mixed uses of the building. Many common IAQ problems are associated with improperly operated and maintained heating, ventilating and air-conditioning (HVAC) systems, overcrowding, radon, moisture incursion and dampness, presence of outside air pollutants, and the presence of internally generated contaminants such as use of cleaning and disinfecting supplies and aerosol products, off-gassing from materials in the building, and use of mechanical equipment. Improper temperature and relative humidity conditions can also present problems, especially concerning comfort.

Many IAQ complaints are associated with flaws in building design and by inadequate routine preventive maintenance of building enclosures (envelopes), plumbing, and HVAC systems (2, 4, 5). To resolve many IAQ problems, a preventive maintenance program should be established based on the system's recommended maintenance schedule outlined by the architect or engineer, the manufacturer, or an HVAC professional. Regular preventive maintenance not only ensures that systems are operating properly, but also can result in cost savings, improved operating efficiency, and

increased worker productivity (6). The U.S. Green Building Council (USGBC), among others, has demonstrated that IAQ issues can be readily and practically addressed when building systems are retrofitted for energy efficiency.
(http://www.usgbc.org/DisplayPage.aspx?CMSPageID=221#v2008)

Benefits of Mitigation of IAQ Problems

Good IAQ in buildings is an important component of a healthy indoor environment. It contributes to a favorable and productive environment for building occupants, giving them a sense of comfort, health, and well-being. Significant increases in worker productivity have also been demonstrated when the air quality was adequate (6). Research has also shown that workers in buildings with adequate air quality have reduced rates of symptoms related to poor air quality (7).

Health Effects

Symptoms related to poor IAQ are varied depending on the type of contaminant. They can easily be mistaken for symptoms of other illnesses such as allergies, stress, colds, and influenza. The usual clue is that people feel ill while inside the building, and the symptoms go away shortly after leaving the building, or when away from the building for a period of time (such as on weekends or a vacation). Health or symptom surveys, such as the one included in Appendix D, have been used to help ascertain the existence of IAQ problems.

Failure of building owners and operators to respond quickly and effectively to IAQ problems can lead to numerous adverse health consequences. Health effects from indoor air pollutants may be experienced soon after exposure or, possibly, years later (8, 9, 10). Symptoms may include irritation of the eyes, nose, and throat; headaches; dizziness; rashes; and muscle pain and fatigue (11, 12, 13, 14). Diseases linked to poor IAQ include asthma and hypersensitivity pneumonitis (11, 13). The specific pollutant, the concentration of exposure, and the frequency and duration of exposure are all important factors in the type and severity of health effects resulting from poor IAQ. Age and preexisting medical conditions such as asthma and allergies may also influence the severity of the effects. Long-term effects due to indoor air pollutants may include respiratory diseases, heart disease, and cancer, all of which can be severely debilitating or fatal (8, 11, 13).

Research has linked building dampness with significant health effects. Numerous species of bacteria and fungi, in particular filamentous fungi (mold), can contribute significantly to indoor air pollution (4, 15-20). Whenever sufficient moisture is present within workplaces, these microbes can grow and affect the health of workers in several ways. Workers may develop respiratory symptoms, allergies, or asthma (8). Asthma, cough, wheezing, shortness of breath, sinus congestion, sneezing, nasal congestion, and sinusitis have all been associated with indoor dampness in numerous studies (21-23). Asthma is both caused by and worsened by dampness in buildings. The most effective means to prevent or minimize adverse health effects is to determine the sources of persistent dampness in the workplace and eliminate them. More details on preventing mold-related problems can be found in the OSHA publication titled: "Preventing Mold-Related Problems in the Indoor Workplace" (17). Other environmental factors such as poor lighting, stress, noise, and thermal discomfort may cause or contribute to these health effects (8).

Sources of Indoor Air Pollutants

The relative importance of any single source depends on how much of a given pollutant it emits, how hazardous those emissions are, occupant proximity to the emission source, and the ability of the ventilation system (i.e., general or local) to remove the contaminant. In some cases, factors such as the age and maintenance history of the source are significant.

Sources of indoor air pollution may include:

Building Site or Location: The location of a building can have implications for indoor pollutants. Highways or busy thoroughfares may be sources of particulates and other pollutants in nearby buildings. Buildings sited on land where there was prior industrial use or where there is a high water table may result in leaching of water or chemical pollutants into the building.

Building Design: Design and construction flaws may contribute to indoor air pollution. Poor foundations, roofs, facades, and window and door openings may allow pollutant or water intrusion. Outside air intakes placed near sources where pollutants are drawn back into the building (e.g., idling vehicles, products of combustion, waste containers, etc.) or where building exhaust reenters into the building can be a constant source of pollutants. Buildings with multiple tenants may need an evaluation to ensure emissions from one tenant do not adversely affect another tenant.

Building Systems Design and Maintenance: When the HVAC system is not functioning properly for any reason, the building is often placed under negative pressure. In such cases, there may be infiltration of outdoor pollutants such as particulates, vehicle exhaust, humid air, parking garage contaminants, etc.

Also, when spaces are redesigned or renovated, the HVAC system may not be updated to accommodate the changes. For example, one floor of a building that housed computer services may be renovated for offices. The HVAC system would need to be modified for office employee occupancy (i.e., modifying temperature, relative humidity, and air flow).

Renovation Activities: When painting and other renovations are being conducted, dust or other by-products of the construction materials are sources of pollutants that may circulate through a building. Isolation by barriers and increased ventilation to dilute and remove the contaminants are recommended.

Local Exhaust Ventilation: Kitchens, laboratories, maintenance shops, parking garages, beauty and nail salons, toilet rooms, trash rooms, soiled laundry rooms, locker rooms, copy rooms and other specialized areas may be a source of pollutants when they lack adequate local exhaust ventilation.

Building Materials: Disturbing thermal insulation or sprayed-on acoustical material, or the presence of wet or damp structural surfaces (e.g., walls, ceilings) or non-structural surfaces (e.g., carpets, shades), may contribute to indoor air pollution.

Building Furnishings: Cabinetry or furniture made of certain pressed-wood products may release pollutants into the indoor air.

Building Maintenance: Workers in areas in which pesticides, cleaning products, or personal-care products are being applied may be exposed to pollutants. Allowing cleaned carpets to dry without active ventilation may promote microbial growth.

Occupant Activities: Building occupants may be the source of indoor air pollutants; such pollutants include perfumes or colognes.

Common Pollutant Categories

Although there are numerous indoor air pollutants that can be spread through a building, they typically fall into three basic categories: biological, chemical, and particle (1).

Biological

Excessive concentrations of bacteria, viruses, fungi, dust mites, animal dander, and pollen may result from inadequate maintenance and housekeeping, water spills, inadequate humidity control, condensation, or water intrusion through leaks in the building envelope or flooding.

Chemical

Sources of chemical pollutants (gases and vapors) include emissions from products used in the building (e.g., office equipment; furniture, wall and floor coverings; pesticides; and cleaning and consumer products), accidental spills of chemicals, products used during construction activities such as adhesives and paints, and gases such as carbon monoxide, formaldehyde, and nitrogen dioxide, which are products of combustion.

Particle (Non-biological)

Particles are solid or liquid, non-biological, substances that are light enough to be suspended in the air. Dust, dirt, or other substances may be drawn into the building from outside. Particles can also be produced by activities that occur in buildings such as construction, sanding wood or drywall, printing, copying, and operating equipment.

Some of the most common indoor air pollutants, and the means to control or prevent them, are discussed in Appendix A.

Prevention and Control of IAQ Problems

IAQ Management Approach

Ideally, an employer should use a systematic approach when addressing air quality in the workplace. The components of a systematic approach for addressing IAQ are the same as those for an overall safety and health program approach, and include management commitment, training, employee involvement, hazard identification and control, and program audit. Management needs to be receptive to potential concerns and complaints, and to train workers on how to identify and report air quality concerns. If employees express concerns, prompt and effective assessment and corrective action is the responsibility of management.

It is recommended that building owners/managers develop and implement an IAQ management plan to address, prevent, and resolve IAQ problems in their specific buildings. The EPA's report, *IAQ Tools for Office Buildings*, provides a set of flexible and specific activities that can be useful to building owners/managers for developing such a plan. A key feature of the plan is the selection of an IAQ Coordinator. The role and functions of an IAQ Coordinator are described in Section 3 of the EPA's report, *IAQ Tools for Schools Action Kit* (24). Other critical features of the plan include establishing necessary IAQ policies, assessing the current status of IAQ in buildings through periodic inspections, maintaining appropriate logs and checklists, performing necessary repairs and upgrades, and implementing follow-up assessments or other needed actions.

Employers who lease space should be familiar with the building management's program and methods for mitigating or resolving indoor air quality problems. It is especially important for employers to know who to contact in buildings where there is mixed use and pollutants are emanating from other sources in the building. Employers should negotiate leases that specify IAQ performance criteria. For example, a lease should specify that the space be ventilated with outdoor air while occupied and at a rate described in ASHRAE 62.1 Ventilation for Acceptable Indoor Air Quality.

An important management strategy is to foster a team approach for problem solving and consensus building. The IAQ Team should include, but not necessarily be limited to, building occupants, administrative staff, facility operators, custodians, building healthcare staff, contract service providers, and other interested parties.

Lastly, following up with affected personnel will serve to validate the effectiveness of the mitigation activities. For more information about the IAQ management approach, refer to OSHA's Safety and Health Topics Page on Injury and Illness Prevention Programs.
(http://www.osha.gov/dsg/topics/safetyhealth/index.html).

Identification and Assessment

Methods used in an IAQ investigation may include identifying pollutant sources, evaluating the HVAC system performance, observing production processes and work practices, measuring contamination levels and employee exposures, providing medical testing or physical examinations, conducting employee interviews, and reviewing records of medical tests, job histories, and injuries and illnesses. The Appendices provide resources and checklists that building owners, managers, and occupants can use to investigate IAQ complaints, document walkthrough inspections, and correct IAQ problems.

To prevent IAQ problems effectively and efficiently, building managers should know and understand the history of the building (construction, uses, maintenance, etc.). If possible, owners and managers should maintain blueprints and construction documents, including information about any renovations of the building.

Some important practices include:

- Inspect and assess the building envelope, including the roof, walls, and foundation, and promptly respond to identified problems. Routinely check the building for water leaks, seals around doors and windows, and any visible damp or moist parts of the building. Clean and dry any damp or wet building materials and furnishings within 24 to 48 hours after detection to prevent the growth of mold.

- Ensure and validate that the building is maintained under a slight positive pressure (i.e., air comes out of the building when exterior doors are opened).

- Check whether the temperature and humidity are maintained in a recommended comfort range (temperature: 68 to 78 degrees and relative humidity: 30% to 60%) (25).

- Ensure that routine maintenance of the HVAC system is being performed, including the performance of the system bringing outdoor air into the building. (1).

- Monitor carbon dioxide (CO_2) levels. The carbon dioxide levels can be used as a rough indicator of the effectiveness of ventilation (5, 26), and excessive population density (e.g., overcrowding).

- Ensure that good housekeeping practices are being applied.

- Ensure that routine preventive maintenance and upkeep of buildings is being performed. A preventive maintenance program provides the care to all building systems and components that keeps them operating at peak performance according to manufacturer's specifications, and also allows for early detection of problems (1, 18).

- Ensure that scheduled renovations are isolated from the building's general dilution ventilation system when occupants are in the building.

Control Methods

There are three basic control methods for lowering concentrations of indoor air pollutants:

1. Source management

Source management includes removal, substitution, and enclosure of sources. It is the most effective control method when it can be applied practically. For example, the U.S. Consumer Product Safety Commission recommends installing carpets that are low-volatile organic compound (VOC) emitters, and encourages consumers to ask retailers or installers about the carpet industry's voluntary "green label" program for new carpets (27). According to the carpet industry, the green and white logo displayed on carpet samples informs the consumer that the specific manufacturer's product has been tested by an independent laboratory and has met the criteria for very low emissions (28). The label, however, is not a guarantee that the carpet will not cause health problems (27). Another example is that the employer can set up temporary barriers or place the space under negative pressure relative to adjoining areas to contain the pollutants during construction activities.

2. Engineering controls

a. Local exhaust
Local exhaust, such as a canopy hood, is very effective in removing point sources of pollutants before they can be dispersed into the building's indoor air.

b. General dilution ventilation
General dilution ventilation systems, when properly designed, operated, and maintained, will control normal amounts of air pollutants. A well-designed and functioning HVAC system controls temperature and relative humidity levels to

provide thermal comfort, distributes adequate amounts of outdoor air to meet the ventilation needs of building occupants, and also dilutes and removes odors and other contaminants. Testing and rebalancing of HVAC systems are essential when partitions are moved in buildings. Appendix C contains an HVAC System Maintenance Checklist that can be used to assist in routine maintenance of the HVAC system. For certain situations, such as painting and carpet cleaning, temporarily increasing ventilation can help dilute the concentration of vapors in the air.

c. Air cleaning

Air cleaning primarily involves the removal of particles from the air as the air passes through the HVAC equipment. Most HVAC system filtration is provided to keep dirt off of coil surfaces to promote heat transfer efficiency. Most smudging observed around air supply diffusers in a ceiling result from entrainment (trapping) of dirt particles in the space that accumulate there because of poor housekeeping.

3. Administrative controls

a. Work Schedule

Through scheduling, managers can significantly reduce the amount of pollutant exposure in their buildings. For instance:

1. Eliminate or reduce the amount of time a worker is exposed to a pollutant (i.e., scheduling maintenance or cleaning work to be accomplished when other building occupants are not present).
2. Reduce the amount of chemicals being used by or near workers (i.e., limit the amount of chemicals being used by the worker during maintenance or cleaning activities).
3. Control the location of chemical use (i.e., perform maintenance work on moveable equipment in a maintenance shop as opposed to the general area, or locate the equipment (e.g., printers, copiers) in a separate room).

b. Education

Education of building occupants regarding IAQ is important (29). If occupants are provided with information about the sources and effects of pollutants under their control, and about the proper operation of the ventilation system, they can alert their employer and/or take action to reduce their personal exposure.

c. Housekeeping

Housekeeping practices should include preventing dirt from entering the environment (using, for example, walk-off mat systems), removing dirt once it is in the building, disposing of garbage, storing food properly, and choosing cleaning products and methods that minimize the introduction of pollutants into the building (18). These steps are outlined in Appendix B.

Seeking Professional Assistance

Some indoor air problems can be resolved when good practices are put in place to control contaminants and building personnel follow good housekeeping approaches. Other problems may be difficult to resolve, however, and may require outside assistance. A building owner or manager may first want to consult local, state, or federal government agencies (e.g., education, health, environmental protection, or agriculture agencies) for assistance or direction in solving IAQ problems. These governmental agencies may be able to help an employer identify the types of experts who could best assist them.

Examples of experts include:

- Structural engineers - address issues with structural elements such as corrosion problems in a building's foundation;

- Architects - responsible for designing the building envelope and can mitigate water intrusion problems by designing vapor barriers;

- Mechanical engineers - test and balance HVAC systems and may be able to assess and recommend repairs/replacement of HVAC systems and local exhaust ventilation systems; and

- Industrial hygienists - assess general IAQ parameters such as air changes in a building, carbon dioxide levels, carbon monoxide levels, and other indoor pollutants, and also evaluate contaminant levels.

There may be private firms or consultants in your area with experience in IAQ work. Such firms may be found in general resources such as a telephone directory (e.g., under "Engineers," "Environmental and Ecological Services," "Laboratories-Testing," or "Industrial Hygiene Consultants"), on the Internet, or by asking building owners/managers for referrals. Some professionals who work with IAQ issues must meet licensing and certification requirements to practice in their disciplines. A consultant should base any testing recommendations or protocol on a thorough visual inspection, walkaround, and interviews with building occupants.

Applicable Standards and Regulations

OSHA does not have a general IAQ standard, but does provide guidelines addressing the most common workplace complaints about IAQ, which are typically related to temperature, humidity, lack of outside air ventilation, or smoking. OSHA standards address potential hazardous conditions leading to serious physical harm or death. Such standards may include those for specific air contaminants, ventilation systems, or the General Duty Clause of the Occupational Safety and Health Act of 1970 (OSH Act). This section highlights OSHA standards, standards interpretations (official OSHA letters of interpretation of its standards), and national consensus standards related to IAQ.

OSHA Standards

All OSHA regulations, interpretations, and the OSH Act can be found on www.osha.gov. Important OSHA statues and standards include:

- Occupational Safety and Health Act of 1970

  Section 5(a)(1), often referred to as the General Duty Clause, requires employers to "furnish to each of his employees employment and a place of employment which are free from recognized hazards that are causing or are likely to cause death or serious physical harm to his employees."

  Section 5(a)(2) requires employers to "comply with occupational safety and health standards promulgated under this Act."

Some of the applicable OSHA Standards are:

- 29 CFR 1904, Recording and Reporting Occupational Injuries and Illnesses.
- 29 CFR 1910.94, Ventilation.
- 29 CFR 1910.1000, Air Contaminants.
- 29 CFR 1910.1048, Formaldehyde.
- 29 CFR 1910.1450, Occupational exposure to hazardous chemicals in laboratories.

Standard Interpretations

- Enforcement policy for respiratory hazards not covered by OSHA Permissible Exposure Limits. (January 24, 2003.)
  https://www.osha.gov/pls/oshaweb/owadisp.show_document?p_table=INTERPRETATIONS&p_id=24749.

- Air monitoring results, citations, and employee exposure records. (March 27, 2002.)
  https://www.osha.gov/pls/oshaweb/owadisp.show_document?p_table=INTERPRETATIONS&p_id=24261.

- The use of ozone gas from ozone generators in a large room. (April 3, 1995.)
  https://www.osha.gov/pls/oshaweb/owadisp.show_document?p_table=INTERPRETATIONS&p_id=21753.

- Request for a list of all OSHA-regulated air contaminants. (March 22, 1995.)
  https://www.osha.gov/pls/oshaweb/owadisp.show_document?p_table=INTERPRETATIONS&p_id=21731.

- Record retention requirements for indoor air quality documents and reports. (August 1, 2002.)
  http://www.osha.gov/pls/oshaweb/owadisp.show_document?p_table=INTERPRETATIONS&p_id=24255.

- Reiteration of existing OSHA policy on indoor air quality: office temperature and environmental tobacco smoke. (February 23, 2003.)
  http://www.osha.gov/pls/oshaweb/owadisp.show_document?p_table=INTERPRETATIONS&p_id=24602.

State Programs

The *Occupational Safety and Health Act of 1970* (OSH Act) encourages states to develop and operate their own job safety and health plans. States with plans approved and monitored by OSHA under section 18(b) of the OSH Act must adopt standards and enforce requirements that are at least as effective as federal requirements. There are currently 27 State Plan states and territories: Twenty-two of these states and territories administer plans covering both private and public (state/territory and local government) workers; the other plans, Connecticut, Illinois, New Jersey, New York, and the Virgin Islands, cover public-sector workers only.

Additional information on State Plans may be found at http://www.osha.gov/dcsp/osp/index.html.

For the most part, these OSHA-approved State Plans adopt standards that are identical to the federal OSHA standards. However, some states have adopted state-specific standards that are at least as effective as the Federal OSHA standards, including the New Jersey IAQ standard. The New Jersey IAQ standard, (N.J.A.C. 12:100-13; 2007) sets standards for indoor air quality in existing buildings occupied by public employees during their regular working hours.

State of California IAQ Program. (http://www.cal-iaq.org/about-us/about-cal-iaq)

This program is a part of the California Department of Public Health (CDPH), separate from the State OSHA program. The purpose of the California IAQ program is to conduct and promote the coordination of research, investigations, experiments, demonstrations, surveys, and studies relating to the causes, effects, extent, prevention, and control of indoor pollution in California.

National Consensus Standards

Note: These are **NOT** OSHA regulations. However, they do provide guidance from their originating organizations related to worker protection.

American National Standards Institute (ANSI)/American Society of Heating, Refrigerating, and Air Conditioning Engineers (ASHRAE).

- **62.1-2010,** Ventilation for Acceptable Indoor Air Quality. This standard specifies recommended outdoor air ventilation rates. The recommended outdoor ventilation rates are based on olfactory studies, and acceptable indoor air quality is met when 80% or more of the exposed people do not express dissatisfaction. Whereas ASHRAE Standard 62 has always been considered a design standard for ventilation, building owner/operators should pay particular attention to Section 8 titled Operations and Maintenance. Section 8 offers guidance to the building owner/operator as to what outdoor air ventilation components should be maintained, what tasks should be performed, and the minimum frequency for performing those tasks.

- **55-2010,** Thermal Environmental Conditions for Human Occupancy. Specifies temperatures that approximately 80 percent of building occupants should find acceptable.

American Society for Testing and Materials (ASTM).

- **E1971–05,** Standard Guide for Stewardship for the Cleaning of Commercial and Institutional Buildings.

OSHA Assistance

OSHA can provide extensive help through a variety of programs, including technical assistance about effective safety and health programs, state plans, workplace consultations, and training and education.

Safety and Health Management System Guidelines

Effective management of worker safety and health protection is a decisive factor in reducing the extent and severity of work-related injuries and illnesses and their related costs. In fact, an effective safety and health management system forms the basis of good worker protection, can save time and money, increase productivity and reduce employee injuries, illnesses and related workers' compensation costs.

To assist employers and workers in developing effective safety and health management systems, OSHA published recommended Safety and Health Program Management Guidelines (54 *Federal Register* (16): 3904-3916, January 26, 1989). These voluntary guidelines can be applied to all places of employment covered by OSHA.

The guidelines identify four general elements critical to the development of a successful safety and health management system:

- Management leadership and worker involvement,
- Worksite analysis,
- Hazard prevention and control, and
- Safety and health training.

The guidelines recommend specific actions, under each of these general elements, to achieve an effective safety and health management system. The *Federal Register* notice is available online at www.osha.gov.

State Programs

The *Occupational Safety and Health Act of 1970* (OSH Act) encourages states to develop and operate their own job safety and health plans. OSHA approves and monitors these plans. Twenty-five states, Puerto Rico and the Virgin Islands currently operate approved state plans: 22 cover both private and public (state and local government) employment; Connecticut, Illinois, New Jersey, New York and the Virgin Islands cover the public sector only. States and territories with their own OSHA-approved occupational safety and health plans must adopt standards identical to, or at least as effective as, the Federal OSHA standards.

Consultation Services

Consultation assistance is available on request to employers who want help in establishing and maintaining a safe and healthful workplace. Largely funded by OSHA, the service is provided at no cost to the employer. Primarily developed for smaller employers with more hazardous operations, the consultation service is delivered by state governments employing professional safety and health consultants. Comprehensive assistance includes an appraisal of all mechanical systems, work practices, and occupational safety and health hazards of the workplace and all aspects of the employer's present job safety and health program. In addition, the service offers assistance to employers in developing and implementing an effective safety and health program. No penalties are proposed or citations issued for hazards identified by the consultant. OSHA provides consultation assistance to the employer with the assurance that his or her name and firm and any information about the workplace will not be routinely reported to OSHA enforcement staff. For more information concerning consultation assistance, see OSHA's website at www.osha.gov.

Strategic Partnership Program

OSHA's Strategic Partnership Program helps encourage, assist and recognize the efforts of partners to eliminate serious workplace hazards and achieve a high level of worker safety and health. Most strategic partnerships seek to have a broad impact by building cooperative relationships with groups of employers and workers. These partnerships are voluntary relationships between OSHA, employers, worker representatives, and others (e.g., trade unions, trade and professional associations, universities, and other government agencies).

For more information on this and other agency programs, contact your nearest OSHA office, or visit OSHA's website at www.osha.gov.

OSHA Training and Education

OSHA area offices offer a variety of information services, such as technical advice, publications, audiovisual aids and speakers for special engagements. OSHA's Training Institute in Arlington Heights, IL, provides basic and advanced courses in safety and health for Federal and state compliance officers, state consultants, Federal agency personnel, and private sector employers, workers and their representatives.

The OSHA Training Institute also has established OSHA Training Institute Education Centers to address the increased demand for its courses from the private sector and from other federal agencies. These centers are colleges, universities, and non-profit organizations that have been selected after a competition for participation in the program.

OSHA also provides funds to nonprofit organizations, through grants, to conduct workplace training and education in subjects where OSHA believes there is a lack of workplace training. Grants are awarded annually.

For more information on grants, training and education, contact the OSHA Training Institute, Directorate of Training and Education, 2020 South Arlington Heights Road, Arlington Heights, IL 60005, (847) 297-4810, or see Training on OSHA's website at www.osha.gov. For further information on any OSHA program, contact your nearest OSHA regional office listed at the end of this publication.

Information Available Electronically

OSHA has a variety of materials and tools available on its website at www.osha.gov. These include electronic tools, such as *Safety and Health Topics*, *eTools*, *Expert Advisors*; regulations, directives and publications; videos and other information for employers and workers. OSHA's software programs and eTools walk you through challenging safety and health issues and common problems to find the best solutions for your workplace.

OSHA Publications

OSHA has an extensive publications program. For a listing of free items, visit OSHA's website at www.osha.gov or contact the OSHA Publications Office, U.S. Department of Labor, 200 Constitution Avenue, NW, N-3101, Washington, DC 20210; telephone (202) 693-1888 or fax to (202) 693-2498.

Contacting OSHA

To report an emergency, file a complaint, or seek OSHA advice, assistance, or products, call (800) 321-OSHA or contact your nearest OSHA Regional or Area office listed at the end of this publication. The teletypewriter (TTY) number is (877) 889-5627.

Written correspondence can be mailed to the nearest OSHA Regional or Area Office listed at the end of this publication or to OSHA's national office at: U.S. Department of Labor, Occupational Safety and Health Administration, 200 Constitution Avenue, N.W., Washington, DC 20210.

By visiting OSHA's website at www.osha.gov, you can also:
- File a complaint online,
- Submit general inquiries about workplace safety and health electronically, and
- Find more information about OSHA and occupational safety and health.

OSHA Regional Offices

Region I
Boston Regional Office
(CT*, ME, MA, NH, RI, VT*)
JFK Federal Building, Room E340
Boston, MA 02203
(617) 565-9860 (617) 565-9827 FAX

Region II
New York Regional Office
(NJ*, NY*, PR*, VI*)
201 Varick Street, Room 670
New York, NY 10014
(212) 337-2378 (212) 337-2371 FAX

Region III
Philadelphia Regional Office
(DE, DC, MD*, PA, VA*, WV)
The Curtis Center
170 S. Independence Mall West
Suite 740 West
Philadelphia, PA 19106-3309
(215) 861-4900 (215) 861-4904 FAX

Region IV
Atlanta Regional Office
(AL, FL, GA, KY*, MS, NC*, SC*, TN*)
61 Forsyth Street, SW, Room 6T50
Atlanta, GA 30303
(678) 237-0400 (678) 237-0447 FAX

Region V
Chicago Regional Office
(IL*, IN*, MI*, MN*, OH, WI)
230 South Dearborn Street
Room 3244
Chicago, IL 60604
(312) 353-2220 (312) 353-7774 FAX

Region VI
Dallas Regional Office
(AR, LA, NM*, OK, TX)
525 Griffin Street, Room 602
Dallas, TX 75202
(972) 850-4145 (972) 850-4149 FAX
(972) 850-4150 FSO FAX

Region VII
Kansas City Regional Office
(IA*, KS, MO, NE)
Two Pershing Square Building
2300 Main Street, Suite 1010
Kansas City, MO 64108-2416
(816) 283-8745 (816) 283-0547 FAX

Region VIII
Denver Regional Office
(CO, MT, ND, SD, UT*, WY*)
1999 Broadway, Suite 1690
Denver, CO 80202-5716
(720) 264-6550 (720) 264-6585 FAX

Region IX
San Francisco Regional Office
(AZ*, CA*, HI*, NV*, and American Samoa,
Guam and the Northern Mariana Islands)
90 7th Street, Suite 18100
San Francisco, CA 94103
(415) 625-2547 (415) 625-2534 FAX

Region X
Seattle Regional Office
(AK*, ID, OR*, WA*)
1111 Third Avenue, Suite 715
Seattle, WA 98101-3212
(206) 553-5930 (206) 553-6499 FAX

* These states and territories operate their own OSHA-approved job safety and health programs and cover state and local government employees as well as private sector employees. The Connecticut, Illinois, New Jersey, New York and Virgin Islands plans cover public employees only. States with approved programs must have standards that are identical to, or at least as effective as, the Federal OSHA standards.

Note: To get contact information for OSHA Area Offices, OSHA-approved State Plans and OSHA Consultation Projects, please visit us online at www.osha.gov or call us at 1-800-321-OSHA.

Appendix A: Common Indoor Air Contaminants

The purpose of this section is to provide additional information about several common indoor air contaminants.

Carbon monoxide (CO)

CO is a colorless, odorless gas produced by the incomplete burning of material containing carbon. CO poisoning[2] can cause brain damage and death. Common sources of CO are leaking vented combustion appliances, automobile exhaust, parking garages, etc. When not properly ventilated, emitted CO can build up. Employees exposed to low levels of CO may feel sick with headache and nausea, and will feel better when exposed to fresh air outside. However, their symptoms will recur shortly after returning to their workplace if CO is not eliminated.

CO Poisoning Symptoms

Poisoning due to low levels of CO can be confused with influenza symptoms, food poisoning, or other illnesses, and can be a long-term health risk if left unattended. Some of the symptoms of low-level CO poisoning are shortness of breath, mild nausea, and mild headaches (30-35).

Prolonged exposure to high levels of CO can lead to brain damage and even death. Adequate ventilation is an important control measure. The OSHA Permissible Exposure Limit (PEL) for CO is 50 parts per million (ppm) as an 8-hour time-weighted average (TWA); the National Institute for Occupational Safety and Health has a Recommended Exposure Limit (REL) of 35 ppm as a 10-hour TWA. According to the American Conference of Governmental Industrial Hygienists (ACGIH), the threshold limit value for CO is 25 ppm as an 8-hour TWA.

Carbon Monoxide Detectors

In addition to having a professional inspect appliances and furnaces, commercially available carbon monoxide detectors can be used to monitor the levels of carbon monoxide in buildings throughout the year. The manufacturer's instructions on placement and maintenance should be followed.

Carbon dioxide (CO_2)

CO_2 is a colorless, odorless, and tasteless gas (36). It is a product of completed carbon combustion and the by-product of biological respiration. ASHRAE states that CO_2 concentrations in acceptable outdoor air typically range from 300-500 ppm. Adverse health effects from CO_2 may occur since it is an asphyxiant gas. At concentrations above 15,000 ppm, some loss of mental acuity has been noted (36). The OSHA PEL is 5,000 ppm as an 8-hour TWA. The CO_2 levels can be used as a rough indicator of the effectiveness of ventilation (26), and excessive population density in a structure. CO_2 increases in buildings with higher occupant densities, and is diluted and removed from buildings based on outdoor air ventilation rates. Therefore, examining levels of CO_2 in indoor air can reveal information regarding occupant densities and outdoor air ventilation rates. High CO_2 levels may indicate a problem with overcrowding or inadequate outdoor air ventilation rates.

Carbon Dioxide Poisoning – Symptoms

CO_2, a by-product of normal cell function, is removed from the body via the lungs in the exhaled air. Exposure to high levels of CO_2 can increase the amount of this gas in the blood, which is referred to as *hypercapnia* or *hypercarbia*. As the severity of hypercapnia increases, more symptoms ranging from headache to unconsciousness appear, and it can also lead to death (36, 37).

Pesticides

Pesticides are any substances or mixture of substances used for preventing, destroying, repelling, or mitigating any pest. These substances include insecticides, herbicides, fungicides, and various other substances used to control pests. Pesticides can cause harm to humans, animals, and the environment because they are designed to kill or otherwise adversely affect living organisms. Pesticides can also kill potential disease-causing organisms (8, 38).

Pesticide Poisoning Symptoms

Symptoms of pesticide poisoning depend heavily on the pesticide to which the worker was exposed. Symptoms often appear within minutes of pesticide exposure, but may take much longer to develop. The most common symptoms include headache, tears in the eyes, vomiting, sweating, and general weakness. Exposure to high doses may cause seizures and death.

---

[2]CO is a chemical asphyxiant; it displaces O_2 in the blood, thereby suffocating the person exposed.

Steps to Reduce Exposure

Integrated Pest Management Principles should always be implemented. Pesticide products should be used according to application and ventilation instructions provided by the manufacturer. In addition:

- Mix or dilute pesticides outdoors;
- Increase ventilation when using pesticides;
- Use non-chemical methods of pest control when possible;
- Do not store unneeded pesticides;
- Dispose of unwanted containers safely; and
- Keep indoor spaces clean, dry, and well ventilated to avoid pest problems.

Radon

Radon is a colorless, odorless, and tasteless radioactive gas (6, 13, 17, 39, 40). It comes from the natural decay of uranium and some other radionuclides that are present in soil. Radon is responsible for most of the public's exposure to ionizing radiation (39, 40). It is often the single largest contributor to an individual's background radiation dose, and levels can vary widely from location to location. Radon gas can accumulate in buildings, especially in confined areas such as attics and basements. Radon penetrates cracks and drain openings in foundations, basements, and crawl spaces. Some building materials will also release radon into the air. It can also be found in some spring waters and hot springs, where it can be released into the air when the water is drawn for use indoors. Exposure to radon may cause lung cancer in humans.

The EPA recommends taking actions to reduce radon exposure if levels exceed four picocuries per liter of air (4 pCi/L) (25). Active soil depressurization and building ventilation are the two most commonly used strategies for controlling radon in buildings. Radon reduction methods include sealing concrete slab floors, basement foundations, and water drainage systems, and increasing ventilation. These techniques are usually cost-effective, and can greatly reduce or eliminate contamination and the associated health risks.

Biological Contaminants

Animals, plants, and microbes are sources of air pollutants. Dander from animals, pollens from plants, and microbes, may act as allergens when they are inhaled. These biological contaminants are usually attached to dust particles of various sizes.

Small dust particles may remain airborne for long periods, while large particles settle more quickly. However, particles that have settled may be easily resuspended in the ambient air by currents of air or other disturbances. Drapery, carpet and other places where dust collects can harbor these contaminants; dirty cooling coils, humidifiers, condensate drains, and ductwork can incubate bacteria and molds. Areas with high humidity can accelerate their growth.

The most common sources of biological air contaminants are moisture-laden areas that support the growth of mold and bacteria present in the air (8, 16, 19, 44). Also, wet surfaces can provide a breeding ground for insects such as dust mites.

Moisture-induced microbial growth can result from water leaks and/or by condensation due to high humidity. Persistent dampness and microbial growth on interior surfaces and in building structures should be avoided or minimized as they may lead to adverse health effects (15). Common sources of moisture in buildings include: plumbing; roof and window leaks; flooding; condensation on cold surfaces, e.g., pipe sweating; poorly maintained drain pans; and wet foundations caused by landscaping or gutters that direct water into or under the building. Water vapor from unvented or poorly vented kitchens, showers, combustion appliances, or steam pipes can also create conditions that promote microbial growth. The most effective means to prevent or minimize adverse health effects is to determine the sources of persistent dampness in the workplace and eliminate them. Also, strict adherence to a housekeeping schedule and use of HEPA-filtered vacuum cleaners will help reduce ambient levels of allergens.

Damp Indoor Environments

Damp indoor environments have been associated with many serious health effects, including asthma, hypersensitivity, and sinusitis. Moisture incursion leading to dampness can result from water leaks and/or by condensation due to high humidity. Common sources of moisture in buildings include: plumbing; roof and window leaks; flooding; condensation on cold surfaces, e.g., pipe sweating; poorly-maintained drain pans; and wet foundations due to landscaping or gutters that direct water into or under the building. Water vapor from unvented or poorly-vented kitchens, showers, combustion appliances, or steam pipes can also create conditions that promote microbial growth.

Well-designed, -constructed and –maintained building envelopes are critical to the prevention and control of excess moisture and microbial growth by avoiding thermal bridges and preventing intrusion by liquid or vapor-phase water. Management of moisture requires proper control of temperatures and ventilation to avoid high humidity, condensation on surfaces, and excess moisture in materials. Ventilation should be distributed effectively in spaces, and stagnant air zones should be avoided (5, 8).

ASHRAE recommends relative humidity levels between 30 and 60 percent for optimum comfort (25). Higher humidity may result in microbial growth. A consistently implemented good-house-keeping plan is essential to eliminate or reduce the microbial growth in the building.

Legionella

Legionellosis or Legionnaires' Disease is caused by a waterborne bacterium, *Legionella*, which grows best in slow-moving, or still warm water (42-44). The primary route of exposure is aerosolization, most commonly from domestic hot-water systems (e.g., showers, sprays, etc.). Mist from evaporative cooling towers without biocide treatment is another reported source. Outbreaks in medical facilities can occur because the patients often have weak or suppressed immune systems.

For cooling towers and evaporative condensers, prevention efforts center on improving the location and maintenance of the cooling towers to limit the growth and spread of *Legionella* bacteria. These devices should be inspected and thoroughly cleaned at least once a year. Corroded parts, such as drift eliminators, should be replaced, and algae and accumulated scale should be removed. Cooling water should be treated constantly with antimicrobial agents. Ideally, an automatic water-treatment system should be used that continuously controls the quality of the circulating water.

For domestic hot-water systems, prevention efforts focus on controlling water temperature, avoiding dead-legs, avoiding stagnation, and cleaning storage tanks to limit the growth and spread of *Legionella* bacteria.

Volatile Organic Compounds (VOCs)

VOCs refer to organic chemical compounds that have significant vapor pressures, and that can adversely affect the environment and human health. VOCs are emitted as vapors from certain solids or liquids, and include a variety of chemicals, some of which may have short- and long-term adverse health effects (17, 45, 46). Concentrations of many VOCs are consistently higher indoors (up to ten times higher) than outdoors. VOCs are emitted by a wide array of products numbering in the thousands. Examples include paints and lacquers, paint strippers, cleaning supplies, pesticides, building materials and furnishings, office equipment such as copiers and printers, correction fluids and carbon-less copy paper, and graphics and craft materials, including glues and adhesives, permanent markers, and photographic solutions (8). More commonly known VOCs include benzene, formaldehyde, methylene chloride, trichloroethylene, and tetra-chloroethylene (13). Exposure to VOCs can result in both acute and chronic health effects, depending on many factors such as the level of exposure and the length of exposure. A few VOCs, such as benzene, have been directly linked to cancer in humans, and others are suspected of causing cancer.

Since people today spend most of their time at home or in an office, long-term exposure to VOCs in the indoor environment can contribute to IAQ re-lated problems (31). In offices, VOCs result from new furnishings, wall coverings, and office equip-ment such as photocopy machines, which can off-gas VOCs into the air (47, 48). Good ventilation and air-conditioning systems are essential to reduce VOC emissions in the indoor environment (47).

Steps to Reduce Exposure
(http://www.epa.gov/iaq/voc.html)

- Use products according to manufacturer's directions.
- Make sure that plenty of fresh air is provided when using these products.
- Discard used containers safely.
- Buy quantities that can be used in short periods of time.

Appendix B: Steps to Improve Indoor Air Quality[3]

What employers can do

- Maintain a good working relationship with building management on indoor environmental issues.
- Place office furniture and equipment in locations based on the adequate air circulation, temperature control, and pollutant removal functions of the HVAC system.
- Coordinate with building management when responsibility for design, operation, and maintenance of the ventilation system is shared.
- Avoid procedures and products that can cause IAQ problems.
- Integrate IAQ concerns into purchasing decisions.
- Work with the building manager to ensure use of only necessary and appropriate pest-control practices; use nonchemical methods when possible.
- Work with building management and the contractor before starting to remodel or renovate to identify ways of minimizing building-occupant exposure, and to ensure that the air-distribution system is not disrupted.
- Encourage building management to develop a preventive IAQ management program following guidance issued by the EPA and the National Institute for Occupational Safety and Health.

What workers can do

- Do not block air vents or grilles.
- Water and maintain office plants properly.
- Dispose of garbage promptly and properly.
- Store food properly.
- Avoid bringing products into the building that could release harmful or bothersome odors or contaminants.
- Notify the building or facility manager immediately if you suspect an IAQ problem.

---

[3]See Item 29 in the last section of this document titled "References."

Appendix C: HVAC System Maintenance Checklist[4]

The following checklist can be used to investigate the HVAC system to make sure it is operating properly (e.g., the right mix of fresh air, proper distribution, and filtration systems are working, etc.)

Cooling Towers

- [ ] Written maintenance and inspection program.
- [ ] Operated in accordance with manufacturer specifications.
- [ ] Inspected regularly (monthly, or as required).
- [ ] Treatment of waste to control microorganisms, as required.
- [ ] Recordkeeping of biocide use – brand, volume, and results.
- [ ] Training of workers for hazards involved.

Humidifiers

- [ ] Written maintenance and inspection program.
- [ ] Inspected weekly during operation.
- [ ] Cleaned and disinfected as required.
- [ ] No visual buildup of mold or slime.
- [ ] Disinfectants removed before reactivating humidifiers.

Cooling Coils

- [ ] Written maintenance and inspection program.
- [ ] Monthly (or, as required) inspections during operation.
- [ ] Removal of dirt, slime, and mold, as required.
- [ ] Upstream filters operating properly.

Drain Pans, drainage systems

- [ ] Written maintenance and inspection program.
- [ ] Monthly inspection (or, as required).
- [ ] Drains maintained in free-flowing condition.
- [ ] No accumulation of stagnant water.
- [ ] No buildup of slime, mold, or dirt.
- [ ] Removal of dirt, slime, and mold, as required.
- [ ] Sample water for microbes, as required.

Duct and Plenum equipment

- [ ] Written inspection and maintenance program.
- [ ] Supply, exhaust, return grilles, and ducts clear and clean.
- [ ] Routine inspection of ducts, debris, and microbial growth (e.g., semi-annually).
- [ ] Provisions of cleanout (e.g., within four feet downstream of duct expansions, supply air openings, or where particulate deposition may occur).
- [ ] Ductwork attached, not dented.
- [ ] Insulation intact, not wet, and no microbial growth.
- [ ] Ductwork properly balanced.

Filtration systems

- [ ] Written maintenance, operating, and inspection programs.
- [ ] Routine inspection.
- [ ] Provision for measuring pressure drops across the filtration system.

---

[4]See Items 24 and 37 in the last section of this document titled "References."

Appendix D: Investigating IAQ Problems and Complaints

Identifying the cause(s) of IAQ problems and complaints may be difficult if an obvious source is not evident. Investigating unclear IAQ problems should take into account patterns and factors, such as occupant complaints and symptoms, location(s) in the building, time of day, seasonal differences, and relationship to activities inside or outside the building. Below are suggestions of information that may be helpful to collect.

Once information is gathered, it should then be analyzed for patterns and possible causes of the IAQ problem. The analysis may point to specific methods, such as those discussed on page 7 (Identification and Assessment). The next step is to fix problems identified and evaluate the results. Has the fix resolved the problems or complaints? If not, then further investigation will need to be pursued. Consultation with safety and health professionals or other experts should be considered at any point during an IAQ investigation.

Information that may be helpful in IAQ investigations:

General office conditions:
- Housekeeping
  - How often is the office vacuumed?
  - How often are carpet and drapes shampooed?
  - How often are floors waxed?
  - Are there any visible signs of dust?
- Have pesticides been applied recently?
- Is there any evidence of moisture intrusion into the building?

Air quality in the office:
- Odor
- Dry
- Humid
- Dusty
- Warm
- Cool
- Drafts
- Temperature fluctuation
  - Within office
  - Between offices
  - Between floors
- Any recent changes in:
  - Work space
  - General office
  - Building
  - New equipment added to the office

When occupant complaints are related to symptoms or health problems, medical evaluation may be required. Persons with respiratory diagnoses that may be caused or exacerbated by workplace exposures should discuss these with their treating physician, and treating physicians may access additional expertise through the network of National Institute for Occupational Safety and Health (NIOSH)-funded Education and Research Centers, or through the member clinics of the not-for-profit Association of Occupational and Environmental Clinics. Workers' compensation systems differ by states, but may also be available to support medical care for work-related diseases.

EPA and NIOSH have published two excellent resources to screen and investigate IAQ problems. The first, published in 1991, is *Building Air Quality: A Guide for Building Owners and Facility Managers* (http://www.cdc.gov/niosh/baqtoc.html). Chapter 6- "Diagnosing IAQ Problems" provides a systematic approach and includes tools, such as logs, questionnaires, diaries, and checklists. The second, published by EPA and NIOSH in 2002, is a companion document that updates and expands on the 1991 publication. The 2002 publication, *Indoor Air Quality Education and Assessment Model (I-BEAM)* (http://www.epa.gov/iaq/largebldgs/i-beam/index.html), is separated into modules, and includes online interactive examples of problems and solutions.

Appendix E: Selected Resources

Hazard Recognition

IAQ problems can be caused by improperly operated and maintained HVAC systems, overcrowding, microbiological contamination, outside air pollutants, and off-gassing from materials in the office and mechanical equipment. Related problems also may include discomfort problems due to improper temperature and relative humidity conditions.

The following references aid in recognizing IAQ hazards in the workplace:

- OSHA Technical Manual. OSHA Directive TED 01-00-015 [TED 1-0.15A] (1999, January 20). https://www.osha.gov/dts/osta/otm/otm_toc.html

- Indoor Air Quality Investigation. Contains guidelines for IAQ investigations, recommendations on sampling instrumentation and methods, as well as guidelines for employers to prevent or alleviate IAQ problems. https://www.osha.gov/dts/osta/otm/otm_iii/otm_iii_2.html

- Carbon Monoxide Poisoning. OSHA Fact Sheet (2002) . http://www.osha.gov/OshDoc/data_General_Facts/carbonmonoxide-factsheet.pdf

- Mold. OSHA Safety and Health Topics Page. https://www.osha.gov/SLTC/molds/index.html

- Stachybotrys Chartarum. OSHA Safety and Health Topics Page. https://www.osha.gov/dts/chemicalsampling/data/CH_267785.html#General

- Indoor Environmental Quality. National Institute for Occupational Safety and Health (NIOSH) Safety and Health Topic Page. Links to several other NIOSH publications, including the NIOSH fact sheet on IEQ. http://www.cdc.gov/niosh/topics/indoorenv

- Preventing Carbon Monoxide Poisoning from Small Gasoline-Powered Engines and Tools. U.S. Department of Health and Human Services, National Institute for Occupational Safety and Health Publication No. 96-118, (1996). Gives examples of the many situations in which people have been poisoned because they did not recognize the danger of using small gasoline-powered engines indoors. These poisonings can occur quickly, even in the presence of what many would consider "adequate ventilation," and in areas that many would define as relatively open spaces, such as parking garages. http://www.cdc.gov/niosh/carbon2.html

- Fact Sheet: Ventilation and Air Quality in Offices. Environmental Protection Agency. Gives an overview of sources of indoor air pollution, health problems and ventilation, control, ventilation standards and building codes, ventilation system problems and solutions, air cleaners, economic considerations, and resolving air-quality problems. http://www.epa.gov/iedweb00/pubs/ventilat.htm

- Air - Indoor Air Quality (IAQ). Environmental Protection Agency. Contains an introduction to IAQ, a listing of common pollutants, and references to IAQ publications, hotlines, and links. http://www.epa.gov/iaq/pubs

- Mold Remediation in Schools and Commercial Buildings. March 2001. Presents guidelines for the investigation, evaluation, and remediation/cleanup of mold and moisture problems in schools and commercial buildings. http://www.epa.gov/iaq/molds/mold_remediation.html

- An Office Building Occupant's Guide to Indoor Air Quality. Describes factors that contribute to indoor air quality and comfort problems, and the roles of building managers and occupants in maintaining a good indoor environment. http://www.epa.gov/iaq/pubs/occupgd.html

- The Inside Story: A Guide to Indoor Air Quality. Office of Radiation and Indoor Air, U.S. Consumer Product Safety Commission. April 1995. Provides a comprehensive online booklet on IAQ concerns in homes. http://www.epa.gov/iaq/pubs/insidest.html

- IAQ Resources. Provides a listing of various hotlines and resources related to IAQ. http://www.epa.gov/iaq/iaqinfo.html

- Guidelines on Assessment and Remediation of Fungi in Indoor Environments. New York City Department of Health. Addresses mold contamination of building components (walls, ventilation systems, support beams, etc.) that are chronically moist or water damaged. http://www.nyc.gov/html/doh/html/epi/moldrpt1.shtml

- Indoor Air Quality Publications. Consumer Product Safety Commission (CPSC). Contains an index of CPSC publications related to IAQ. http://www.cpsc.gov/cpscpub/pubs/iaq.html

Evaluation and Control

Methods used in an IAQ investigation may include: identification of pollutant sources; evaluation of HVAC system performance; observation of production processes and work practices; measurement of contamination levels and employee exposure; medical testing or physical examinations; employee interviews; and review of records of medical tests, job histories, and injuries and illnesses.

The following resources provide information about evaluating and controlling IAQ in the workplace.

Evaluation

- Volatile Organic Compounds in Air. OSHA Method PV2120. May 2003. https://www.osha.gov/dts/sltc/methods/partial/pv2120/pv2120.html

- Ozone in Workplace Atmospheres (Impregnated Glass Fiber Filter). OSHA Method ID-214. March 1995. https://www.osha.gov/dts/sltc/methods/inorganic/id214/id214.html

- Carbon Monoxide in Workplace Atmospheres (Direct-Reading Monitor). OSHA Method ID-209. March 1993. https://www.osha.gov/dts/sltc/methods/inorganic/id209/id209.html

- Sulfur Dioxide in Workplace Atmospheres (Impregnated Activated Beaded Carbon). OSHA Method ID-200. April 1992. https://www.osha.gov/dts/sltc/methods/inorganic/id200/id200.html

- Carbon Monoxide in Workplace Atmospheres. OSHA Method ID-210. March 1991. https://www.osha.gov/dts/sltc/methods/inorganic/id210/id210.html

- Formaldehyde in Workplace Atmospheres (3M Model 3721 Monitor). OSHA Method ID-205. December 1990. https://www.osha.gov/dts/sltc/methods/inorganic/id205/id205.html

- Carbon Dioxide in Workplace Atmospheres. OSHA Method ID-179. June 1987. https://www.osha.gov/dts/sltc/methods/inorganic/id172/id172.html

- For additional information, see OSHA's Safety and Health Topics Pages on:
  - Formaldehyde https://www.osha.gov/SLTC/formaldehyde/index.html
  - Hazardous and Toxic Substances https://www.osha.gov/SLTC/hazardoustoxicsubstances/index.html
  - Legionnaires' Disease https://www.osha.gov/SLTC/legionnairesdisease/index.html
  - Sampling and Analysis https://www.osha.gov/SLTC/samplinganalysis/index.html
  - Styrene https://www.osha.gov/SLTC/styrene/index.html

- EPA: IAQ Tools for Schools Action Kit. http://www.epa.gov/iaq/schools/actionkit.html

- The National Institute for Occupational Safety and Health (NIOSH), through its Health Hazard Evaluation (HHE) Program, responds to requests from employers, employees and their representatives, and government agencies. NIOSH conducts workplace assessments to determine if workers are exposed to hazardous materials or harmful conditions, and whether these exposures are affecting workers' health. NIOSH has conducted more than 200 IAQ-related HHEs. Recent reports can be found on NIOSH's Indoor Environmental Quality website at http://www.cdc.gov/niosh/topics/indoorenv

- Department of Energy. Guide to Operating and Maintaining EnergySmart Schools. Building Technology Program. U.S. Department of Energy. Office of Energy Efficiency and Renewable Energy. http://apps1.eere.energy.gov/buildings/publications/pdfs/energysmartschools/ess_o-and-m-guide.pdf

- GSA 2003 Facilities Standards (P100) Overview. Environmental Policies & Practices. http://www.gsa.gov/portal/content/101230

- U.S. Green Building Council LEED for Existing Buildings. Leadership in Environmental and Energy Design for Existing Buildings. http://www.usgbc.org/DisplayPage.aspx?CMSPageID=221#v2008

Control

- A Brief Guide to Mold in the Workplace. OSHA Safety and Health Information Bulletin. October 10, 2003. https://www.osha.gov/dts/shib/shib101003.html

- Ventilation. OSHA Safety and Health Topics Page. https://www.osha.gov/SLTC/ventilation/index.html

- Building Air Quality: A Guide for Building Owners and Facility Managers. U.S. Department of Health and Human Services, National Institute for Occupational Safety and Health (NIOSH) Publication No. 91-114. Also, referenced as Environmental Protection Agency (EPA) Publication No. 400/1-91/003. December 1991. http://www.cdc.gov/niosh/baqtoc.html

- Building Air Quality: Action Plan. Publication No. 98-123. Also, referenced as EPA Publication No. 402-K-98-001. June 1998. Provides an 8-step building air-quality action plan for building owners and managers to be used with NIOSH Publication No. 91-114 and EPA Publication No. 400/1-91/033. http://www.cdc.gov/niosh/98-123a.html

Appendix F: OSHA-Sponsored Environmental Tobacco Smoke Workshops

Workshop I

Workshop Summary: Assessing Exposure to Environmental Tobacco Smoke in the Workplace. Jonathan M. Samet. *Environmental Health Perspectives Supplements*, vol. 107, no. S2, May 1999.

Environmental tobacco smoke (ETS) is a term now widely used to refer to the mixture of sidestream smoke and exhaled mainstream smoke that pollutes air in locations where tobacco smoking is taking place. A multidisciplinary workshop was convened to address key issues related to ETS exposure in the workplace in order to prepare the groundwork for a risk assessment of the hazard ETS poses to workers. Workshop participants concluded that substantial evidence was now available on worker exposure to ETS using both direct and indirect approaches to exposure assessment, and that these data could be used to project distribution of exposures to ETS in the nation's workplaces. This summary of the discussions at the workshop is an overview of the suggested approach to exposure assessment.

http://ehpnet1.niehs.nih.gov/docs/1999/Suppl-2/309-312samet/abstract.html

Workshop II

OSHA/ACGIH® Environmental Tobacco Smoke Workshop Proceedings, Publication #99-078

Proceedings of the OSHA/ACGIH® Environmental Tobacco Smoke Workshop held June 6, 1998, in Cincinnati, OH. The workshop brought together a panel of ventilation experts, along with hospitality industry managers and design engineers, to discuss effective and non-effective ventilation strategies for smoking sections in restaurants and bars.

Workshop III

Workshop Summary: Workshop on Health Risks Attributable to ETS Exposure in the Workplace. Maritta S. Jaakkola and Jonathan M. Samet (Johns Hopkins University, Baltimore, Maryland, USA). *Environmental Health Perspectives*, vol. 107, supp. 6, December 1999.

This 1998 workshop was convened to address the health risks of exposure to environmental tobacco smoke (ETS) in the workplace. It was paired with a 1997 workshop on issues related to ETS exposure in work environments. The 1998 workshop involved a multidisciplinary group of participants who reviewed evidence on the quantitative risks to health posed by ETS and discussed the development of risk assessment methodology for the future.

References

1. U.S. EPA. An Office Building Occupant's Guide to Indoor Air Quality.
    http://www.epa.gov/iaq/pubs/occupgd.html

2. U.S. EPA. Indoor Air Quality. The Inside Story: A Guide to Indoor Air Quality.
    http://www.epa.gov/iaq/pubs/insidest.html

3. CDC. Healthy Housing Reference Manual. Chapter 5: Indoor Air Pollutants and Toxic Materials.
    http://www.cdc.gov/nceh/publications/books/housing/cha05.html

4. NIOSH Recommendations for the Cleaning and Remediation of Flood-Contaminated HVAC Systems: A
    Guide for Building Owners and Managers. http://www.cdc.gov/niosh/topics/emres/Cleaning-Flood-HVAC.html

5. American Society of Heating, Refrigerating and Air-Conditioning Engineers (ASHRAE) (2010). ASHRAE
    Standard 62.1. Ventilation for Acceptable Indoor Air Quality. Atlanta, GA.

6. Fisk, W.J. (2000). Health and Productivity Gains from Better Indoor Air Environments and Their Rela-
    tionship with Building Energy Efficiency. Annual Review of Energy and the Environment, 25: 537-566.

7. Spengler, J. D., Samet, J. M., and McCarthy, J. F. (2001). Indoor Air Quality Handbook. McGraw-Hill.

8. U.S. EPA. An Introduction to Indoor Air Quality (IAQ).
    http://www.epa.gov/iaq/ia-intro.html#Indoor%20Air%20Pollution%20and%20Health

9. American Thoracic Society. Environmental Controls and Lung Disease. American Review of
    Respiratory Disease, 1990, 142: 915-939.

10. American Lung Association. Health Effects and Sources of Indoor Air Pollution, Parts I and II, 1989,
    Publication No. 0857C. http://www.indoorpollution.com/air_pollution.htm

11. European Concerted Action. Indoor Air Quality & Its Impact on Man. Environment and Quality of Life.
    Report 10. Effects of Indoor Air Pollution on Human Health (1991).

12. U.S. EPA. Indoor Air Pollution: An Introduction for Health Professionals. (Last updated April 28, 2010).
    http://www.epa.gov/iaq/pubs/hpguide.html

13. Bernstein, J. A., Alexis, N., Bacchus, H., Bernstein, I. L., Fritiz, P., et al. (2008). The Health Effects of
    Nonindustrial Indoor Air Pollution. Journal of Allergy and Immunology, 12(3): 585-590.

14. Stapczynski, J.S., 2004. Chapter 62: Respiratory Distress. Tintinalli, J.E., Kelen, G.D., Stapczynski, J.S.,
    Ma, O.J., and Cline, D.M. Tintinalli's Emergency Medicine, 6th Edition.

15. World Health Organization (WHO) (2009). WHO Guidelines for Indoor Air Quality: Dampness and Mould.
    http://www.euro.who.int/__data/assets/pdf_file/0017/43325/E92645.pdf

16. CDC Online Source for Credible Health Information: Mold. http://www.cdc.gov/mold

17. OSHA. Preventing Mold-Related Problems in the Indoor Workplace. OSHA 3304-04N 2006.
    http://www.osha.gov/Publications/preventing_mold.pdf

18. CDC. Healthy Housing Reference Manual. Chapter 5, Indoor Air Pollutants and Toxic Materials.
    http://www.cdc.gov/nceh/publications/books/housing/cha05.html

19. U.S. EPA. IAQ Building Education and Assessment Model (I-BEAM): TIA Maintenance and
    Housekeeping Programs.
    http://www.epa.gov/iaq/largebldgs/i-beam/text/maintenance_and_housekeeping.html#IAQ%20Housekeeping%20Tasks

20. OSHA. A Brief Guide to Mold in the Workplace. OSHA Safety and Health Information Bulletin, October
    10, 2003. http://www.osha.gov/dts/shib/shib101003.html

21. Institute of Medicine (IOM) (2004). Damp Indoor Spaces and Health. Washington, DC: National
    Academy of Sciences.

22. Fisk, W. J., Lei-Gomez, Q., Mendell, M. J. (2007). Meta-analysis of the Associations of Respiratory
    Health Effects with Dampness and Mold in Homes. Indoor Air 17(4):284-296.

23. World Health Organization (WHO) (2009). WHO Guidelines for Indoor Air Quality: Dampness and
    Mould. WHO Regional Office for Europe.
    http://www.euro.who.int/__data/assets/pdf_file/0017/43325/E92645.pdf

24. U.S. EPA. Indoor Air Quality. Tools for Schools Action Kit IAQ Coordinator's Guide: A Guide to Implementing an IAQ Program. http://www.epa.gov/iaq/schools/tools4s2.html

25. ASHRAE Standard 55 (2010). Thermal Environmental Conditions for Human Occupancy.

26. ASTM Standard D-6245-98. Using Indoor Carbon Dioxide Concentrations to Evaluate Indoor Air Quality and Ventilation.

27. U.S. Consumer Product Safety Commission. Tips for Purchasing and Installing New Carpet. CPSC Document #454. http://www.cpsc.gov/cpscpub/pubs/454.html

28. Carpet and Rug Institute (1999). Carpet and Indoor Air Quality Technical Bulletin. http://www.carpet-rug.org/technical_bulletins/9902_Carpet_and_IAQ.pdf

29. NIOSH. Building Air Quality: Action Plan. http://www.cdc.gov/niosh/baqact4.html

30. U.S. Consumer Product Safety Commission. The Senseless Killer. 1993 GAO Publication No. 1993-0-356-764.

31. Mott, J. A., Wolfe, M. I., Alverson, C. J., Macdonald, S. C., Baily, C. R., Ball, L. B., et al. (2002). National Vehicle Emissions Policies and Practices and Declining U.S. Carbon Monoxide Mortality. JAMA, 288: 988-995.

32. American Lung Association. Carbon Monoxide Indoors. http://www.lungusa.org/healthy-air/home/resources/carbon-monoxide-indoors.html

33. U.S. EPA. An Introduction to Indoor Air Quality: Carbon Monoxide. http://www.epa.gov/iaq/co.html

34. OSHA. Carbon Monoxide Poisoning. Fact Sheet, 2002. 2 pages. http://www.osha.gov/OshDoc/data_General_Facts/carbonmonoxide-factsheet.pdf

35. OSHA. Carbon Monoxide in Workplace Atmospheres. OSHA Method ID-210, March 1991. http://www.osha.gov/dts/sltc/methods/inorganic/id210/id210.html

36. Health Canada. Indoor Air Quality in Office Buildings. Carbon Dioxide. http://www.hc-sc.gc.ca/ewh-semt/pubs/air/office_building-immeubles_bureaux/co2-eng.php

37. Canadian Centre for Occupational Health and Safety. Health Effects of Carbon Dioxide Gas. http://www.ccohs.ca/oshanswers/chemicals/chem_profiles/carbon_dioxide/health_cd.html

38. U.S. EPA. An Introduction to Indoor Air Quality: Pesticide. http://www.epa.gov/iaq/pesticid.html

39. U.S. EPA. A Citizen's Guide to Radon. The Guide to Protecting Yourself and Your Family from Radon. EPA 402/K-09/001. January 2009. http://www.epa.gov/radon

40. Agency for Toxic Substances and Disease Registry (ATSDR). Radon. September 2008. CAS ID #: 14859-67-7. http://www.atsdr.cdc.gov/substances/toxsubstance.asp?toxid=71

41. OSHA. Mold. Safety and Health Topics Page. http://www.osha.gov/SLTC/molds/index.html

42. Canadian Centre for Occupational Health and Safety. Legionnaires Disease. http://www.ccohs.ca/oshanswers/diseases/legion.html

43. CDC. Legionellosis Resource Site (Legionnaires' Disease and Pontiac Fever). Patient Facts: Learn More about Legionnaires' disease. http://www.cdc.gov/Legionella/patient_facts.html

44. OSHA. Legionnaires' Disease. Safety and Health Topics Page. http://www.osha.gov/SLTC/legionnairesdisease/index.html

45. OSHA. Volatile Organic Compounds in Air. OSHA Method PV2120, May 2003. http://www.osha.gov/dts/sltc/methods/partial/pv2120/pv2120.html

46. U.S. EPA. An Introduction to Indoor Air Quality: Volatile Organic Compounds (VOCs). http://www.epa.gov/iaq/voc.html

47. Yu, C. and Crump, D. (1998). A Review of Emission of VOCs from Polymeric Materials Used in Buildings. Building and Environment, 33(6): 357-374.

48. Hrigaray, P., Newby, J. A., Clapp, R., Hardell, L., Howard, V., et al. (2007). Lifestyle-Related Factors and Environmental Agents Causing Cancer. An Overview. Biomedicine and Pharmacotherapy, 61(10): 640-658.